Shepherding
In the
African American Community

While every precaution has been taken in the preparation of this book, the publisher assumes no responsibility for errors or omissions, or for damages resulting from the use of the information contained herein.

SHEPHERDING IN THE AFRICAN AMERICAN COMMUNITY - PASTORAL CARE CONVERSATIONS

First edition. February 18, 2024.

Copyright © 2024 Willie A. Glaster, Jr..

ISBN: 979-8224689286

Written by Willie A. Glaster, Jr..

Table of Contents

Rev. Willie A. Glaster

Volume II

Other books by Willie A. Glaster, Jr.

Shepherding in the African American Community, Vol. I
A Diamond Journey by William Allan
Poems of Personal Growth and Spirituality: The Sounds
Of Black Voices

ACKNOWLEDGMENTS

I wish to, currently, acknowledge those who have made an impact upon me, both spiritual and personal. First, I thank God for this opportunity. Next, I express my sincerest love of my wife, Anita, whom for so many years had to put up with cluttered desks and other stuff. I applaud her for who she is now and the future. Next, I want to thank Everett, whom over the past five years had to endure delayed gratification. Your encouraging words over the past few months mean more to me than words can ever imagine. To, Gilbert, whom is now a married man, thanks for letting Dad "practice" his parenting skills. I love you all very much from the bottom of my heart.

Sincere thanks go to Rev. Dr. LaJoyce Lawton, Pastor of Barnett Chapel, United Methodist Church, Kerrville, Texas, and her congregation for allowing me to do this final project. Next, I want to thank my pastor, Rev. Dr. Charles F. Johnson, Senior Pastor of Trinity Baptist Church, San Antonio, Texas, for his unwavering encouragement, exhortation and support of Anita and me. I have dearly missed you over the past months. Thanks to the Kerrville Library Staff and the Kerrville Historical Society for their assistance during the final days. Thank you, Lackland Chapel, for helping me discover my place in ministry. Thank you, faculty of Wayland Baptist University. To all of my friends, theological students, Bible Study participants, and co-workers, who have shared in this amazing journey of life.

Finally, I am grateful to the faculty and staff of Oblate School of Theology. To Dr. R Scott Woodward for his mentorship and wise counsel. You all have poured into me so much that words cannot truly express my deepest appreciation. May Our Lord and Our God abundantly bless and keep you.

Special Notes: All Scripture in the report is from the New Revised Standard Version of the Bible, unless noted otherwise.

Barnett Chapel News: In the November 15, 2018 issue of The Hill Country Community Journal, Kerrville's Hometown Newspaper, the city celebrated the 121-year history of Kerrville's Barnett Chapel Methodist Church. The Church was formally recognized Saturday morning during a Texas historical marker dedication ceremony as the oldest African American Church in Kerr County.

This Book was adapted from the master thesis by Willie Glaster called:

EVANGELISM IN SOUTH TEXAS:
A PASTORAL PERSPECTIVE IN AN
AFRICAN AMERICAN CHURCH

Introduction

Evangelism in the twenty-first century and beyond is a call and challenge for the African American in our post-modern world, and specifically for the Black church in South Texas. Modernity beckons the African American to break ties with its history, a history that is intricately tied to liberation of the past and present. As we look toward our future, the Kingdom of God will have to be retold in a way that awakens the souls of an exiled people. The wave of crises in this century lies within the fact that a large number of Black churches are closing its doors around the country, just recently in New Orleans. The same fate is being felt in the Black churches in South Texas. The effective witness of the Gospel is the challenge and measure for the small church.

This is a final project that will report on the historical perspective of a particular small church of sixty members and the theological basis for evangelism, in relation to the distinctiveness of pastoral ministry at Barnett Chapel, Kerrville, Texas. The church's pastor, Rev. LaJoyce C. Lawton, requested that I come and assist, as a pastoral intern. On January 8, 2006, Rev. Lawton, presented to her congregation, during the 2006 Church Meeting, plans to implement four areas, which were: stewardship, evangelism, care and concerns ministry, and the formation of ministry teams.

Each month during the Administrative Council meetings, Ministry Teams will report their progress in evaluation of meeting the 2006 goals and objectives. Also, during this internship, I had the task of instructing an Evangelism course for five students participating in the Certificate In Theology program, offered by the Interdenominational Theological Center.

I endeavor to demonstrate my spiritual giftedness, academic and pastoral training through application of different ecumenical methodologies. These methodologies will be a study and exploration of the demographics adjacent to Barnett Chapel; to discover, minister, and witness to people of the Kerrville community through intentional outreach; and to engage the members of this church through effective teaching, training, and preaching.

Historical/Social Perspective

If one were to ponder the historical view of Barnett Chapel, it would be wise to understand the other influences within the city that led to the church's inception. William E. Montgomery, in an article commenting on the African American churches, had this to say: "African Americans who entered Texas from the 1820's through the Civil War years generally did so as slaves. In this country they developed a faith born from the union of African traditions and Christian evangelism... By the time owners and traders began transporting slaves to Texas, however, distinctively African American patters of worship evolved. Most slaves had some form of contact with organized Christian churches and merged the ideas they learned there with what they remembered individually or collectively from Africa...

Other masters, in light of the Christian-based militant abolitionist movement, sought pragmatically to supervise the slaves' religious instruction in order to filter the subversive messages from the Christian Gospel. They wanted slaves to hear that God expected them to obey their masters and not steal from them...How slaves responded to this type of worship varied from one individual to the next, but in most cases, they preferred churches of their own and preachers who also were slaves" (Montgomery 1).

As told in the Handbook of Texas Online, "By 1860, Kerr County had a population of 634, including 49 black slaves. While one plantation owner owned twenty-one slaves, the remainder of the slaves were scattered among thirteen slave owners". Dr. Charles Ganahl owned the largest number of slaves. Dr. Ganahl, in 1861, assessed he had owned 21 slaves, valued at $12,000. When the slaves were freed by President Lincoln's Emancipation Proclamation, many slaves established homesteads just south of Center Point. An oral tradition involving the story of Theodore Blanks' last name is pivotal in the legacy of Blacks in Kerrville. It is said that Mr. Blanks asked Dr. Ganahl for his reparations, now that he was a freed man.

Dr. Ganahl denied his request by stating that he would give him *"nothing"*, which Theodore translated to mean "I am nothing"; thus, the history of the name "Blanks".

In 1892, a small band of black Christian settlers, in particular several people from the Robinson, Buckner, Butler, and Blanks families, began having community services that were held from house to house. By 1897, there were still no churches for Blacks in Kerrville. These worshippers began having services in a school used by Mexican Americans. Other Black families, who belonged to other Methodist traditions, moved to Kerrville and joined the small group of congregants, in the area known as "The Settlement". The first church was a single room structure, which was built by the Thornton,

Benson, Ware and Barney families around 1900. From the scant historical data available on Barnett Chapel, there have been three buildings erected in or around the site as it is presently known. As I searched the information, l was surprised to find no record of baptisms, conversions to faith and attendance figures.

Let us now turn our attention to another portion of the historical perspective that deals with the review of the famous document presented by W.E. B. DuBois, entitled "The Negro Church" at the Atlanta Conference in 1903. DuBois' report to the conference is a result of a ten-year investigation from 1890 to 1900 of African American churches and conferences throughout the United States. This report notes that any study of social life, economic cooperation, and education among blacks must begin with the church. The study reveals the importance of the church on society, in this fashion:

> "The Negro Church is the only social institution of the Negroes which started in the African forest and survived slavery under the leadership of priest or medicine man, afterward of the Christian pastor, the Church preserved in itself the remnants of African tribal life and became after emancipation the center of Negro social life. So that today the Negro population of the United States is virtually divided into church congregations which are

the real units of race life (DuBois ii). By 1890, the number of churches and organizations in the state of Texas totaled approximately 4,500 with memberships nearing 190,000 people. In the closing address of the Atlanta Conference the report had the following to say about the Negro church: "I have seen the Negroes in all their religious moods, in their most death-like trances and in their wildest outbreak of excitement. ..They may be more emotional than ethical... They are remarkable here than anywhere else; their religion has had more to do in shaping their better character in this country than any other influence; it will most determine what they are to become in their future development" (DuBois 214).

If one were to take a broader view of the Negro churches at the turn of the twentieth century, there are several noticeable facts that hindered the means of evangelism, which were reported by H.K. Carroll: Early tendencies toward race segregation; later tendencies toward race cooperation; the failure of mere charity; and the Negro ability to organize and rule. The disadvantage here was separating friends, helpers, and co-religionists. Political inexperience and lack of teachers was the culprit. In some of the remarks concerning Texas ministers, the main concerns were sexual immorality and financial dishonesty. The final component of the investigation made available by this report dealt with 1,339 children in the Atlanta public schools, between the ages of seven to eighteen years of age. The first inquiry asked the children: *Are you a Christian?* 494 of the children responded "Yes" and nearly double of that amount replied **"No"**. Nearly sixty percent of the children 11 -18 years of age belonged to no church. The next two probing questions were: *Do you go to church, and do you like to go to church?* The highest number of children who responded positively was between the ages of 10 to 13 years old. And finally, the research revealed this statement:

> "The children of twelve and under had the clearer and simpler idea of the direct connection of goodness and Christianity, while older children tended more toward
>
> phrases which sought to express the fact that religion had reference to some higher power, this was the more popular idea, and 70 per cent of the children spoke of Christianity as "Love for God," "Belief in Christ" are such phrase. Clear as such phrases may be to some minds, they undoubtedly point to a lack in the moral training of many children. They evidently are not impressed to a sufficiently large extent with the fact that moral goodness is the first real sign of a Christian life". (DuBois 189).

We shall move forward to the last subsection that pertains to the social perspective, which will be the challenge of the African American church in the twenty first century. If one shall follow closely, the challenge of the African American church today in the broader sense will be reflected at the local level as well-in particular Barnett Chapel. The first challenge is gender disparity. Jawanza Kunjufu, author of, *Adam! Where Are You? Why Most Black Men Don't* Go *to Church,* makes us aware of the problem by observing the following factors: For the male church membership population-the average adult men total is 70, with the average male youth is 29, bringing the total to 99. In contrast, the average adult women is 199, with the average number of female youth is 77, bringing the total female population to 291. Thus, the female population represents 75 percent of the African American church, with the male population representing 25 percent. He points out that despite the unexplainable disparity, this problem could be the result of unemployment, racism, and other societal factors. For the African American church to make an impact in the community, it will have to increase the percentage of males and youth (Kunjufu 16).

The next challenge comes in the education of African American pastors. In this area, Kunjufu make this alarming statement: "...it is estimated that only 10 percent-20 percent of the clergy nationwide have completed their professional education at an accredited divinity school or theological seminary. Despite an increasing number of pastors who are pursuing their college education as they take their ministry more seriously, in years past, it has been estimated that as many as 80 percent of African American pastors who had been called were not trained...We would not allow that of doctors, dentists, lawyers, accountants, or teachers; but we do allow that of our ministers" (18-19). T. Vaughn Walker and Robert Smith, Jr, in their essay, on "Christian Ministry in the African American Church: A Challenge For Seminarians and Seminaries", reported "the African-American church must be challenged to produce proactive and scholarly contributions to the academy...It is the seminary that will inspire, encourage, and train such gifted researchers and writers for leadership in the academy ... " (Gushee & Jackson 327)

The third challenge of the African American church lies with the ability of the pastor to preach. Kunjufu categorizes the Black church in three ways that represent the character of the preaching-entertainment, containment, and liberation. The author says that the entertainment church "makes you feel good for the moment but does not address societal issues. The church administrators may have activities during the week, but they do not empower their congregation". Containment churches are similar to the entertainment church except, as Kunjufu explains: "they are open from 11 a.m.-1p.m. on Sundays and closed the remainder of the week". The final church that Kunjufu addresses is the one that preaches liberation, where people understand that the Cross is both vertical and horizontal. I may add here that the African American church preacher must observe two fundamental convictions about preaching, as given to us by Fred B. Craddock, author of the book, *Preaching:* "One is that the minister works within an unusual network of trust and intimacy that makes the separation of character from performance impossible ... The second observation is that all preaching is to some extent self-disclosure by the preacher... It is simply a truth about communication"... (Craddock 23). He or she may also need to remember or review Thomas G. Long, in his book, *The Witness of Preaching.*

> Bearing witness to the gospel means engaging in serious and responsible biblical preaching. Preaching is biblical whenever the preacher allows a text from the Bible to serve as the leading force in shaping the content and purpose of the sermon. More dynamically, biblical preaching involves telling the truth about bearing witness to-what happens when a biblical text intersects some aspect of our life and exerts a claim upon us... Biblical preaching happens when a preacher prayerfully goes to listen to the Bible on behalf of the people and then speaks on Christ's behalf what he or she hears there... (Long 48)

The very core of successful reflection in preaching must be in the area of powerful transformation, as stated in the book, *Naming Grace,* by Mary Hilkert. Preaching must connect people with the presence of God and thus "draws the hearers of the word into a deeper relationship with God that is at the same time a deeper experience of their everyday human life and relationships as graced" (33). In all honesty, many of the Black congregations in South Texas, are not faced with a provoking crisis, or an unsettling gospel. What we are left with is a one-verse rendition of how pastors deal with troublesome congregants. Usually, the deacon will rush to grab a metal chair and then place it in front of the altar, to usher in the invitation to Christian discipleship. Thus, we are left pondering the question-"What gospel is that?" (40).

Kunjufu conducted a comprehensive study of over 75 Black men at a subsequent retreat, trying to understand the disparity among Black men and church. For this paper, I look at three of the twenty-one issues raised by his study. The three are spirituality/ worshiping alone, evangelism, and irrelevance. The following comments shared in the retreat was this "I believe in God. I don't necessarily know what to call Him...I don't know if He died on the cross and rose from the dead...I don't feel a need to have to go to a church, to a building, to male pastor, and pay my 10 percent admission of all my earnings to do right... I'm the block club president. Some brothers in church don't do anything on the block...I want to live right, but I don't need structure, nor do I need other people around me to believe in God"... (68). The evangelism issue on the questionnaire was, "Have you ever been witnessed to?" The sad commentary about this issue revealed that only one person out of the seventy-five men had ever been witnessed to. His feelings posed the question that "Did Jesus die only for the middle class?" (69). The last issue spoke about irrelevance. The major problems facing the African American community are crime, drugs, teen pregnancy, unemployment, and single parenting. The respondents felt that the church was not responding to the issues.

Furthermore, they would rather listen to Minister Louis Farrakhan or attend a conference or workshop than go to church (60)

James Cone, author of *A Black Theology of Liberation,* vividly expresses the foundation for black theology in five sources, which are: experience, history, culture, revelation, scripture, and tradition. In experience, African Americans want to know what Jesus Christ means when they are confronted with the brutality of any form of oppression. Cone expressed this: "The black experience prevents us from turning the gospel into theological catch phrases and makes us realize that they must be clothed in black flesh" (23-24).

SHEPHERDING IN THE AFRICAN AMERICAN COMMUNITY - PASTORAL CARE CONVERSATIONS

The poet Langston Hughes puts it this way when referring to the black experience in the poem *The Negro Speaks of Rivers*:

I've known rivers: I've known rivers ancient as the world and older than the flow of human blood in human veins.

My soul has grown deep like the rivers.

I bathed in the Euphrates when dawns were young. I built my hut near the Congo and it lulled me to sleep. I looked upon the Nile and raised the pyramids above it. I heard the singing of the Mississippi when Abe Lincoln went down to New Orleans, and I've seen its muddy bosom tum all golden in the sunset. I've known rivers; Ancient, dusky rivers.

My soul has grown deep like the rivers.

Regarding black revelation, read what W.E. 8. DuBois had to say, from his book, *The Souls of Black Folks*:

After the Egyptian and Indian, the Greek and Roman, the Teuton and Mongolian, the Negro is a sort of seventh son, born with a veil, and gifted with second sight in this American world,—a world which yields him no true self-consciousness, but only lets him see himself through the revelation of the other world. It is a peculiar sensation, this double-consciousness, this sense of always looking at oneself through the eyes of others, of measuring one's soul by the tape of a world that looks on in amused contempt and pity. One ever feels his twoness, -an American, a Negro; two souls, two thoughts, two unreconciled strivings; two warring ideals in one dark body, whose dogged strength alone keeps it from torn asunder.

With that in mind, how do we bridge the gap to find relevance in our history and the Christian witness? The hope lies within the scope of the next section, the theological basis.

The Theological Basis for Evangelism

In this section of the report, I will attempt to focus primarily on three aspects for a theological basis for evangelism, which will be: the theological issues of evangelism; a need for a theological response; and how do I view ministry as a pastoral response to evangelism. We will begin with the issues facing evangelism. Walter Brueggemann, who authored the book, *Biblical Perspectives on Evangelism: Living in a Three-Storied Universe,* stated in the opening paragraph that there is a "deep crisis facing the church. On the surface, there is a drive for survival as mainline churches noticed diminished membership diminished dollars and eroding influence and importance. Below that surface agenda, there is the growing awareness among us of the resistance of our culture to the primary claims of the gospel" (Brueggemann 7). Dr. Martin Luther King, Jr., in his biography, *Why We Can't Wait.* brings another point that looks at the crisis facing the church by stating "if today's church does not recapture the sacrificial spirit of the early church... it will be dismissed as an irrelevant social club with no meaning for the twentieth century (King 96). Recently, I drove through a community in San Antonio, only to be shocked to find the deplorable conditions of a war zone-like neighborhood.

There were four predominantly African American churches located within a two-to-three block radius; each one representing the disfigurement of the community. The churches have not responded in a way that exemplified the transforming salt and light of the earth.

Brueggemann mentions in the opening chapter of three implications of evangelism; however, for the report there will be only two mentioned here. The first he terms as a dichotomy between evangelism and social action. If evangelism is taken and we leave out social action, as he admits, "we are left with the question, "News for what?" (43). The author goes on to say that if we take social action as the feature, one is left with the question, "Social action from what source and for what end?" (43) It is here that Brueggemann challenges the reader to realize the answer comes from the "radical news of God's new governance over the world, and social action is witness and praise to the new governor. Any social action, which is not rooted in the news and aimed at the new ruler, has no claim upon biblical warrants" (43).

> The second implication of evangelism is found in its relation to church growth.

His stance purports that evangelism is never focused primarily on institutional enhancement. The simple claim of evangelism is to summon people to a new, liberated obedience to God. This is how he explained it: "The church is a modest gathering locus for those serious about the new governance. There must be such a gathering, and such a meeting, and such a community, because the new governance is inherently against autonomy, isolation, and individualism" (45). When the mirror is held to the Black church, in particular, the implication is greater. In James H. Cone's book, *Speaking the Truth,* the reader will find several views on the problem of liberation focused solely on institutional enhancement:

> Do Black churches, as institutions, still regard black people's struggles for political liberation as the theological foundation of their *raison d'etre?...To* worship together as a community, persons must live together in community, and to live together as one people of God, white and black Christians must believe and as if God has given them an identity that transcends the human barriers designed to separate them...Denominationalism is a disease that makes black church people more concerned about their Baptist, African Methodist Episcopal, African Methodist Episcopal Zion, or Pentecostal identity than they are about proclaiming and living the gospel of Jesus (Cone 82)..

Is there a solution to this challenge? Perhaps, there is, if we focus on two ingredients, as suggested by Bruggemann-"first, we must recover gospel modes of discourse which are not moralistic, dogmatic, scholastic, or piestic, but relentlessly dramatic. Second, we must recover the focal drama of baptism, which is a subversive act of renunciation and embrace ...The crisis concerning evangelism is a "world question" and not a "church question" (Bruggemann 45-46).

Any evangelistic effort, as an activity of the church, must be first rooted in the Gospel, the good news. Evangelism, at the very core, is defined as declaring the Gospel to the unregenerate. Someone might ask then, what is an unregenerate person? Primarily, if one were to look at the prefix-un-one would discover that it expresses a reversal of the action or separation. Next, observe the word, regenerate, as defined in Webster's Dictionary-to give fresh life or vigor to; to reorganize; to recreate the moral nature; to cause to be born again; born anew; changed from a natural state to a spiritual state. Where do we find the true source, for the African American church, concerning evangelism?

We find the source of evangelism lies within the framework of the New Testament as it declares God's action to save the world in and through His Son, Jesus the Christ. William Thompson reminds us to remember: "Jesus Christ is God's good news because his life, death, and resurrection make salvation available to all, both the Jewish people and the Gentile world. Thompson demonstrates the transformation of the phrase, good news, in this fashion: "Good news", translates "gospel," which derives from the Anglo-Saxon "god-spell," "good tidings." It also translates the Greek *euangelion*, "good tidings," and *euangelizesthai*, to "announce good news." These terms in the **NT** are no doubt influenced by the Hebrew *bsr* and its derivatives as used in Isaiah 40:9; 41:27; 52:7 to designate the good news of the salvation to Zion, and especially in Isaiah 61:1, which describes the same salvation as comforting the afflicted and releasing captives" (Thompson in Stuhlmueller 392). Let's move further in our discovery into the Synoptic Gospels.

Mark introduced his interpretation of the story of Jesus by calling it "The beginning of the good news of Jesus Christ, the Son of God" (Mark 1:1). At the beginning of Jesus' Galilean ministry, Mark states this in 1:14-15-"Now after John was arrested, Jesus came to Galilee, proclaiming the good news of God, and saying, "The time is fulfilled, and the kingdom of God has come near; repent, and believe in the good news." Next, we find following Mark's Gospel, as told to us by Burton Throckmorton in the *Gospel Parallels,* is

Matthew, specifically in the preaching journey in Galilee, in Matthew 4:23-"Jesus went throughout Galilee, teaching in their synagogues and proclaiming the good news of the kingdom and curing every disease and every sickness among the people" (Throckmorton xxxiv). Thus, as Thompson eloquently summarizes Jesus' work in Galilee: "He preaches, heralds, proclaims the good news that God has seized power and has begun his definitive rule over the world. As preacher, Jesus announces God's action in the world; as teacher, he will speak of what people are to do, how they are to live in the light of that good news (5:1-7:28), as healer, he will reveal God's rule over evil in the world (8:1-9:34)" (Stuhlmueller 394). In the rejection at Nazareth narrative, we read in Luke's gospel, 4:16-19-When he came to Nazareth, where he had been brought up, he went to the synagogue on the Sabbath day, as was his custom. He stood up to read, and the scroll of the prophet Isaiah was given to him. He unrolled scroll and found the place where it is written: "The Spirit of the Lord is upon me, because he has anointed me to bring good news to the poor. He has sent me to proclaim release to the captives and recovery of sight to the blind, to let the oppressed go free, to proclaim the year of the Lord's favor". Luke repeatedly uses the verb "bring good news to describe Jesus' ministry and summarize the activities with the verb "proclaim" as its synonym. Thus, Jesus' mission in Luke's account is threefold: preaching good news to the poor, proclaiming release to captives, and preaching the good news of God's reign (Thompson in Stuhlmuller 395).

The next source of evangelism is found in the function of the Holy Spirit, in particular, Acts. Luke, who is the author of Acts as well as the Gospel according to Luke, gives the account of the ascension scene of Jesus Christ to Theophilus. It is in Acts 1:8, that we find Jesus promises to his apostles the gift of the Holy Spirit and the spread of their witness to the ends of the earth-"But you will receive power when the Holy Spirit has come upon you; and you will be my witnesses in Jerusalem, in all Judea and Samaria, and to the ends of the earth". Augustine Stock, in his commentary on *Witness,* the Greek words *martyrs* and *martyria* plays a crucial role for anyone to understand evangelistic witnessing. For this, the apostles were given a special gift of the Holy Spirit. The Spirit would inspire them about what they would say when they were brought before the tribunals. The Spirit is a witness with them and gives them strength and courage with which they gave their testimony (Stock in Stuhlmueller 1087). Thus, in the true sense, life, and death rests in the balance of a true witness's testimony.

What is the biblical scope of evangelism for the Black church? This scope lies within four major areas: to all nations, house-to-house, always being prepared, and as ambassadors. In the Gospel of Matthew, written to a community of Greek-speaking Jewish Christians who were internally disrupted, Matthew 28:18-20 reads: And Jesus came and said to them, "All authority in heaven and on earth has been given to me. Go therefore and make disciples of all nations, baptizing them in the name of the Father and of the Son and of the Holy Spirit, and teaching them to obey everything that I have commanded you. And remember, I am with you always, to the end of the age". There are several factors that shape African American theology when we discuss evangelism. James Cone, in his work, *A Theology of Black Uberation,* talks about a fifth source, which is Scripture. He informs the reader the importance of Scripture to black theology in the following manner: "By taking seriously the witness of scripture, we are prevented from making the gospel into private moments of religious ecstasy or into the religious sanctification of the structures of society...Efforts to prove verbal inspiration of the scriptures result from the failure to see the real meaning of the biblical message: human liberation! While churches are debating whether a whale swallowed Jonah, the state is enacting inhuman laws against the oppressed. It matters little to the oppressed who authored scripture; what is important is whether it can serve as a weapon against oppressors" (31). The King James Version of the Song of Solomon, 1:5-6, summarizes the great heart of Scripture in this powerful way:

"I am black, but comely, O ye daughters of Jerusalem, as the tents of Kedar, as the curtains of Solomon. Look not upon me, because I am black, because the sun hath looked upon me; my mother's children were angry with me; they made me the keeper of the vineyards; but mine own vineyard have I not kept. One of the great theologians of our time, Georgia Harkness, a Methodist, recommends three important steps in her book, *Understanding the Christian Faith:*

There is no more searching question than anyone can ask than the one which the Philippian jailer put to Paul, "What must I do to be saved?" Paul's answer, "Believe on the Lord Jesus Christ," is bedrock for Christian faith and experience ...But even when one knows that he ought to be a follower of Christ and see that through Christ others find a power that transforms their living, the question remains as to how to enter into this experience... The first step is awareness of need... The awareness of need which is essential to the finding of God comes most often, if not always, through a human agency...The stimulus that awakens us to our own need may be a book, a sermon, a service of worship... In short, the thing that wakes us up can be anything that shows the difference Christ makes in the lives of persons who place him at the center of their faith and loyalty. This awareness of need can come at any time, during the smoothest existence or the stormiest. We are especially open to this discovery when something occurs to upset our familiar pattern of life-a great new responsibility, such as marriage, parenthood, or a new vocation; an emergency, such as failure, illness separation by physical absence or death from someone that is loved. Even our hardest experiences and darkest hours, as many found during the strains of war, can be avenues of the discovery of our own need and availability of God's limitless power.

The second step, growing out of the first without clear separation, is surrender of will. The term "surrender" sounds strange to modern ears, for it reflects a mood at variance with the prevailing mental climate. We want to be masters of our fate and captains of our souls-that is, if we still believe there is a soul of which to be captain. The idea of surrendering to anybody or anything suggests servility, and we do not want to be servile..."Being religious" means subjecting man's will to the will of God.

The third step has already been mentioned. This is deliverance. This third step, like all the others, is one in which openness of spirit must be joined with active effort. God delivers but delivers only those who will accept what is offered. God saves the person who is "lost," but only him who is willing to find the way... It means reorganization of life from the inside out, and from the bottom up. Failure to recognize this fact has

led to the gruesome practice of counting the number of souls saved in meetings, and it has helped to fill church rosters with people whom the rest of the world call hypocrites.

The fourth step, therefore, is spiritual growth... The person who achieves most fully the experience which has been described will be the last to boast of being a Christian. But others will all him this and will see in him a living witness to the power of Christ, who is "the author and perfecter of our faith"... These are the steps which need to be taken today if we are to find power in God to grapple with the problems of our time.

How do I see evangelism as a pastoral response? In the Black church today, there is debate about the term "soul-winning" as a substitute of evangelism. "Soul winning" is a term which may easily obscure the role of God in salvation and misinterpret man's role. We do not save souls or win them; we witness to the One who alone is able to save. Frank Stagg, in his book, *New Testament Theology,* realizes the potential danger in the impoverishment of the term "soul". Stagg remarks "in the New Testament "souls" are persons (cf. Luke 12:19f; Acts 2:41,43; Romans 13:1; Revelation 6:9). Salvation is not concerned with some mere extraction or separable part of a person. "Soul" in this sense is a Greek idea, not a biblical one. A soul is a self' (Stagg-269).

A further investigation into the possible problem of substitution evangelism, from a pastoral response perspective, is to observe varying forms of evangelism, which are: the ecclesial and the pietistic. Samuel Southard and Anita Ostrom wrote the essay, entitled, *"Evangelizing"*, which is found in the *Dictionary of Pastoral Care and Counseling*. "The ecclesial perspective assumes the church itself as mediator of the Word through preaching, worship, and sacrament, and in the fellowship of believers. From this perspective, evangelism emphasizes calling persons into the whole life of the church as the medium through Christ is known and discipleship to Him is formed. The event of evangelism is viewed as a gradual and social process. The pietistic approach, on the other hand, while focusing on subjective, experiential knowledge, assumes that evangelism leads one toward a direct, unmediated and personal encounter with Jesus Christ that leads to a surrendering of the self to Him in act of explicit, conscious decision and commitment" (Southard in Hunter 375). In the pietistic approach, because of the critical evaluation of the human sciences and a distrust of natural processes in matters of faith, is viewed as more theologically conservative, thus leading to tension between the two approaches. As a pastoral response, we must recognize that the secular school of psychology is often critical of evangelism, due to the rules of private, state, and federal institutions. If evangelism is to readily acceptable in our buildings, then training of counselors in the pastorate is very important.

Paul Tillich wrote in the 1956 symposium on Evangelism and Pastoral Psychology, that the evangelist cannot ask how we communicate the gospel so that others will accept it, for there is no method. To communicate the gospel means putting it before the people so that they can decide for or against it. Our purpose is to enable others to make a genuine decision, to witness to the way in which we have made this decision and why it is necessary for a decision to be made. In times of stress or change in adult life may be opportunities for evangelism. These life transitions become the occasion for joining a church on the part of persons who have been Christians by name but are now open and willing to hear the gospel message (Southard in Hunter 377). St. Augustine, whom I discovered during my theological studies, was Black, more precisely an African, is considered the great example of the classical Christian viewpoint regarding his conversion experience.

Southard found out there were four aspects of counseling during his studies, in successful revivals, revealed the following: an open concern for people; diligent pastoral care; responsible fellowship; fervent personal and practical preaching. He later discovered that a revival makes an enduring impact upon individuals when revivals are closely associated with the work of pastors and Christian fellowships (378).

Southard & Ostrom, concluded in their final analysis, these areas: "Sociologists point out that with the rise in secularization and pluralism in modern Western culture there is an undermining of external authority structures and an increase of voluntarism in church membership...While a theological judgment needs to be made about this in itself, the larger question facing evangelists concerns the meaning and method of evangelism in the twentieth century. What is the place of faith, the role of decision and the nature of commitment in this era of increased communication and mobility, rapid change, and cultural pluralism with its attendant diffusion of the lines of authority?" (379)

As I begin to move forward to the process and analysis section of the report, I close the pastoral response and recommendation by observing the challenges that lie ahead. Peter J. Paris reflects on the challenges the Black church must face by saying: "Further research on the psychology of oppressed peoples both as victims and as agents of liberation can help black theology in its reflections" (Paris et al Hunter 100). The capacity to transcend the conditions of oppression and the self-initiating activities of Black people along with the capacity to undergo them represent two poles of the experience that must not be separated from each other (100).

How do I, as an African American, see evangelism as a

pastoral response in ministry? I bring to Barnett Chapel, a predominantly Black, United Methodist Church, a person whose life experiences has been changed through the demonstration of God's love and compassion for me, acknowledging that I am a sinner, believing in His Son, Jesus the Christ and accepting the free gift of God's grace. I came to Barnett Chapel understanding who I am in Christ, albeit from an ecumenical perspective. I come with an understanding of my African American and Indian heritage, coming from a lower lower sub-society in Valdosta, Georgia. I discovered, because of my conversion experience took place in a rural evangelical church, that my culture places the experience in a lower social class. I bring to this body of believers knowing that although I lived in the city, a rural-minded standard was present. Valdosta's geographical line was identified by a railroad track. I come with knowledge that my political, religious, social and economic status is dictated in the lower-lower social class if you are Black and lived on the "Southside". With that in mind, the next area of discussion is the pastoral context.

The pastoral implication in preaching is vast and very crucial to both the congregation and preacher. For us to understand our role in preaching, we need to know and identify with the people to whom they are speaking. Like a shepherd in the field, we, as under-shepherds, are called to be

sensitive, concerned, and knowledgeable of the struggles, doubts, and joys of the member of the local community. However, the black church needs to consider the community in which she exists-it is one of constant change in demographics. The challenge for black preaching is to hear from different communities in its geographic location. Hilkert calls for the preacher, in the life of community, to be a pastoral theologian, not an academic or professional theologian.

> "All of life", as stated by Hilkert, is the appropriate
> subject for the pastoral reflection (140).

In response to African American pastoral care, one must understand the pattern of agape, or unconditional love, as developed by Black Christians who understood themselves to be related significantly to God. It is this liberating worldview that God is intimately involved in black people's lives, caring for them and sustaining them in the midst of oppression and racism. It is within this context that this form of ministry seeks to elicit a response to God's immanent activity through values, symbols, and methods of care. Edward Wimberly states, from a historical perspective, five key structures are within the black church. These structures are: the symbolic worldview, the role of the black preacher, the family, the extended family, and the church as a support system (92). These systems when conversion is experienced by the black person, it reflects the quality of

God's care for them.

I have come to recognize and appreciate the symbols in the Black church: the brush arbor, the mourning bench tradition, and the mutual aid societies that were the support structures used primarily as vehicles of reconciliation, where people found wholeness, hope, forgiveness, and love. The brush arbor was a secret supportive religious meeting held by slaves where they sought to worship God freely. The mourning bench tradition, which is still operative in some churches today, was a place or location in the church, usually in the front, where people were aware of God working in their lives convicting them of sin and drawing them to salvation. The mutual aid societies were support systems formed during slavery and the reconstruction period to assist persons to maintain physical, emotional, social, economic, and spiritual well-being through caring relationships in the face of life and crises such as death, dying, bereavement, and loss.

Goals. Objectives, and Evaluation

This report now takes us to a point, after reviewing the theological basis for evangelism, are the goals and objectives that were set for this internship in relation to the activities performed in this project.

BARNETT CHAPEL UMC EVANGELISM TASK FORCE PLANNING SHEET

DATE: January 28, 2006

NEEDS ANALYSIS: "Therefore go and make disciples of all nations, baptizing them in the name of Father and of the Son and of the Holy Spirit." *Matthew 28:19*

GOAL: In 2006, we will increase membership at Barnett Chapel UMC by adding **90** new believers and/or unchurched people by Easter.

OBJECTIVES: To bring the unsaved and unchurched into this Body of Christ called Barnett Chapel.

1. To study and explore the target area adjacent of Barnett Chapel.
2. To gather and compile information on all unsaved and unchurched persons of the community.
3. To discover, minister and witness to people of the community through intentional outreach programs.
4. To instruct and prepare new members of the uniqueness of Barnett Chapel that will move them toward becoming an active congregation.

ACTIVITIES:

1. Develop a list of individuals/couples in the **30, 40, 50 yr. old - age group** who are not members of a church.
2. Recruit **three (3)** people from the congregation that will be on the **Evangelism Task Force.**
3. 25 church members shall identify **90** people as stated in #1 above. (Research show

that **one (1)** believer knows at least **eight (8) unchurched** *people-Evangelism Planning Handbook* by Suzanne Brader, General Board of Discipleship UMC, Section on Evangelism, 1987).

SECTION 2

1. Conduct intercessory prayer for the people identified.
2. Conduct Evangelism training during one or two Bible Study sessions in late February, or early March.
3. Do intentional outreach to the unchurched in the community.
4. Help believers share the good news of Jesus Christ.
5. Review progress and report findings in February, March, and 1st Sunday in April.
6. Assess the community; find out the needs of those through door-to-door visitation; hand out invitation and door hangers/knockers *(Purchase from Outreach.com or Cokesbury Bookstore).*
7. Evaluate current method of information compilation of new church visits.

8. Train Lay leadership on procedures to process a new member into Barnett Chapel.
9. Examine and explore outreach, mentorship and enrichment opportunities that will equip and strengthen the unity of Barnett Chapel.

SHEPHERDING IN THE AFRICAN AMERICAN COMMUNITY - PASTORAL CARE CONVERSATIONS

There were three Bible Study sessions on Evangelism at Barnett Chapel; these sessions were conducted on March 8th, 15th, and 22nd. A total of 20 people attended these sessions. The topics discussed were:

Session One- An Introduction

A Importance of Prayer in Evangelism

8. Why Evangelism? A look at statistics and U.S. Census demographics as it related to evangelistic opportunities in Kerrville.

C. Are You Saved? A review of Scripture in relation to salvation-Romans 3:20-31, 4:4, 10:9-13; Matthew 3:2; Acts 82:38, 8:36-38, 16:31; Luke 13:3; John 3:16-18;

IJohn 1:9; Ephesians 2:8-10.

Session Two-Evangelism is for everybody (Psalm 51:10-13 and II Corinthians 5:17)

A. Exercise on Witnessing for Christ
B. Witness: Telling Your Story.
C. Overcoming weaknesses in telling the Good News

Session Three-Objections and Excuses Why People Don't Receive Jesus Christ

A. A look at 15 reasons and a biblical response to the

reasons

A. Methods that hinder Evangelism.
B. Basic comparisons of Christianity with other cults and religions

As I reviewed the 2000 U.S. Census report for Kerrville, the following social characteristics stood out while I prepared for the Bible Studies:

A. Out of 20,425 people, almost 2,900 people have a 9th grade education or less.
B. 2,122 widowed and divorced women.

A. 700 grandparents are responsible grandchildren.
B. 30% of population has household income less than $25,000.
C. 650 families live below poverty level.
D. 15% household type are female, no husband, and with children under 18 years.
E. Racial makeup: White-75%; Hispanic-22%; Black-3%.

Evaluation of the Bible Studies revealed the following remarks:

A. Participants felt that they received excellent biblical responses to their questions.
B. Congregation was enlightened concerning information on the different religions as compared to Christianity.
C. Folder contents made it easier to share information with other Christians, especially friends.
D. Congregation acknowledged need for support concerning education, outreach to widowed and divorced women, grandparents raising grandchildren.

A. Congregation felt encouraged, by way of biblical support, when people objected to the Good News.
B. They appreciated that I was a very capable, well-informed and educated teacher.

The following is a brief look at the attendance at Barnett Chapel during the practicum. January 15th-36 total (4 visitors); January

22nd-57 (31 visitors); January 29th-43 (one visitor); No totals for February 5- 19 due to weather; February 26th-44 (no visitors); March Sth-44 (no visitors); March 1ih_37 (two Visitors); March 19th-18 (two visitors); March 26th-36 (0 visitors); April 2nd-22 (0 visitors). Therefore, we had approximately 45 visitors come to church.

The other training session that took place was the Evangelism Course for students that are participating in the Certificate in Theology program. The classes took place at St. Paul's United Methodist Church, San Antonio, Texas, from January 12 - February 23, 2006. There was a total of five students who completed this course. The areas covered in this course are outlined below:

Week One-An Introduction

Why Evangelism?

Review of Chapter One from Walter Brueggemann's *Book-Biblical Perspectives on Evangelism.*

Eight elements of the Gospel-Good News foretold (Acts 2:16-21; 3:12-13). Fulfillment of prophecy (Acts2:22,25-31; 3:18,22-6). Jesus' death for our sins (Acts 2:23; 3:15). Jesus' resurrection from the dead (Acts 2:24-32; 3:15). Presence of the Holy Spirit (Acts 2:33-36, 38; 3:19). Call to repentance (Acts 2:37-39; 3:19). Forgiveness of sins (Acts 2:38; 3:19). God's ultimate victory (Acts 2:33; 3:21).

Are You Saved? Romans chapter 3

Our Heart's Desire-Romans 1O:1-15

Everyone has a God-sized emptiness (Five examples) Attempts to fill emptiness; Success as a substitute for God; Work as a substitute for God; Cult involvement as a substitute for God; The quest to find true meaning of a life fulfilled.

WILLIE A. GLASTER, JR.

<u>Week Two-What is Evangelism?</u> (I John 4:14-15; Acts 1:8).

Seven Excuses Churches Use for Not Evangelizing

<u>Week Three-Objective in Evangelism</u> (Acts 8:26-40)

Discussed Chapter Two from Brueggemann's book.

Joshua 24-Outsiders become Insiders; Retelling the Story; Who's Invited; Lives Redescribed; Covenant; Story-Based Imperatives.
<u>Week Four-Witnessing for Christ</u>
Review of Chapter Three from Brueggemann's book (Forgetting and Remembering).
The Believer as a witness
Review of Objections/Excuses as to why people don't receive Jesus Christ (from the Billy Graham Christian Life & Witness Course).
Eight unchurched people I know (Family members, neighbors; work/school; and other friends).
<u>Week Five-Planned Evangelism</u> (from the book, Leadership **<u>Handbook of Outreach and Care</u>**); Review of the Spiritual Gift of Evangelism
<u>Week Six-Youth Becoming Belief-ful Adults.</u>

Review of Chapter Four from Brueggemann's book (Beloved Children becoming Belief-ful Adults); Why should we be "crazy" about the young? What's the meaning (Exodus 12:29; 13:8.14); Narratives which command (Deuteronomy 6:4-9); What are the God stories? Telling A PasUOreaming A Future (Psalms

78:5-8; Joel 2:28-29; Acts 2:17-18); What is the requirement for everyone concerning evangelism?

Brief look at Hispanic Evangelism and a review of the U.S. Census Report concerning the students' church location.

WILLIE A. GLASTER, JR.

<u>Course Evaluation</u> by the students of the Interdenominational Theological Center-San Antonio campus revealed my strengths and weaknesses:

A. Created atmosphere of love and acceptance in the group-Excellent.
B. Encouraged group participation-Excellent.
C. Supported group members-(3) Excellent, (1) Good.
D. Prepared to lead group sessions-(3) Excellent, (1) Good.
E. Maintained a positive attitude and sensitive to activity of the
    a. Holy Spirit-(3) Excellent, (1) Good.
F. *<u>When asked about what they appreciate most about the</u>* Created *<u>instructor,</u>* they said: "His passion for what he was doing and his level of knowledge; attentive and inclusive to every class member; was prepared with resources conductive to class study".
G. *<u>When asked about what kinds of activities were most meaningful,</u>* their response: "The breaking down of topics in subtopics, the time spent in discussing each subtopic; willingness to allow members to share how they applied ideas in class reinforced practical learning".
H. *<u>When asked if they could choose one item they would want to spend more time in class,</u>* they stated: "Prayer and sharing of testimonies more; actual witnessing; more search of Scripture, implementing effective strategies and methods".
I. *<u>When asked what adjustments they sensed God was</u>*

leading them to make, they stated: "To become more diligent in organization; prioritizing my time; continued development of a deeper prayer life; reading and studying of God's Word; return to the basics and the Great Commission; rebirth of lost passion; remembering the call into ministry".

Conclusion

African Americans have experienced uprooting from their ancestral home in Africa, nearly four centuries of survival against all odds, a quest for elevation, and a continuous pursuit after liberation. Evangelism is no safe church activity that will sustain a conventional church, said Walter Brueggemann. Upon reflection about this practicum, I have come to the same conclusion. Any church, particularly the Black church, will not be able to maintain the status quo or maintain heritage solely on tradition; and if she does, she will lose the effective herald of her witness-her symbolic bell will toll no more. In the Black church, we all face an uphill challenge to help awaken the soul from slumber, to renew the faculties of remembering, to train our youth to become believers in Jesus Christ. Conversion and the transformation are the keys to a spirit that is still caught in the bondage of slavery-slavery of the mind. We must hear the Good News, or we will everything else. Without transformation, the African American church will eventually fade into a oblivion, to become a footnote on the American landscape. We too, as a people, could become like our European brethren and sisters who failed to capitalize on the evangelistic proclamation of the good news of the previous century.

I have learned that constant training and teaching is needed, regardless of our denominational endeavors. When we relegate ourselves to remind people that state laws prohibit the presence of firearms on Black church premises, we are then at the first stages of decay. I have learned that our souls long for a place to call home. We must remember always that our home is with God. The One who invites us to sit at his table; it is already set. It is here that we find our joy and peace. We discover that the stories are to be retold again. We now become the storytellers who will retell the stories for the young ones to hear. The contributions of the Black church are enormous, and we must remember it. If we continue to retell the good news of a God who has liberated us through His Son Jesus Christ, then people, such as the great German theologian Dietrich Bonhoeffer, though our worship and proclamation, and allowing the Holy Spirit to move on the hearts and minds of teenagers like Georgia Harkness, who later became a powerful theologian in her own right, then we will be the effective witness God intended His people to be.

- THE AUTHOR

APPENDIX A:

HANDOUTS USED FOR EVANGELISM TRAINING AT BARNETT CHAPEL UMC

The Soul Winner's Travail: A biblical example

Factors That Influence Evangelism

Satan: The Obstacle Who Hinders

Are You Saved? Are You Saved?[2] & The Result of Salvation

Session One: The Introduction

Session Two: The Soul Winner

Session Three: Reasons Why People Don't Receive Jesus Christ Objections and Excuses

Methods that Hinder Evangelism

Satan: A Defeated Foe

THE SOUL WINNERS TRAVAIL:
A Biblical Example

A REGULAR PASSION FOR SOULS, *My heart is broken and I am in great sorrow (Romans 9:2).*

o Continual brokenness (heaviness) and sorrow (heartbreak). Paul said in Acts 20:31- *"Be on your guard! Remember how day and night for three years I kept warning you with tears in my eyes".* In Hebrews 5:7, we learn that Jesus Christ was a Man of *"strong c1ying and tears ".* Isaiah 53:3 announced He was a fan of *"sorrows and acquainted with grief".*

o From the Gospel accounts, we learn that Jesus wept over **individuals** (John 11:33- 35), over **crowds** (Mark 6:34; Matthew 9:36; 14:31); over **cities** (Matthew 23:37-38).

THE SOUL WINNER'S TRIALS: WINNING THE CONVERT

FOUR CLASSES OF PEOPLE FROM THE BIBLE.

o **The religionist.** Paul said this: *"When I am with the Jews, I live like a Jew to win Jews. They are ruled by the Law of Moses, and I am not. But I live by the Law to win them. (2IJ And when I am with people who are not ruled by the Law, I forget about the Law to win them.*

Of course, I never really forget about the law of God. In fact, I am ruled by the law of Christ". (I Corinthians 9:20-21). <u>An illustration of this point is made in Acts 16:1-3.</u>

□ **The moralists-those ruled by the law.** (See the Scripture printed above from I Cor. 9:20). <u>An illustration of this point is provided in Acts 21:17-26.</u>

The worldings, those not ruled by the law (i.e., secular, carnal, sorbid, proud, unspiritual),

Scripture printed above from I Cor. 9:21). <u>An illustration of this point is provided in Acts 17:16-34.</u>

SUFFERING 'WITH' CHRIST

The precious service of leading the enlightened person to a decision is often appointed to the one who has first suffered for that person in intercession (prayer).

□ Need of great clearness and skill in explaining exact terms of the Gospel to the

one upon whom the Spirit is moving in conviction.

□ Plan of salvation should be clearly understood, and those texts and passages kept in mind which are adapted to meet the mental confusion that Satan produces in those with whom the Spirit is dealing.

Above all, the personal worker (witness) must be wholly dependent upon the leading of the Spirit.

□ Should be prepared to do the unusual thing as the usual.

☐ If really prepared for service, **his or her ear will be open to God** concerning every person he or she may chance to meet but will not assume to force a decision without divine direction.

☐ A personal decision should be pressed *only when so led by the Spirit.*

All true service for God is the ministry of the Spirit through the believer.

☐ Compassion for lost souls will be created in the heart **by the Spirit.**

☐ **Holy Spirit** will answer intercessory prayer by going forth through ministry of the Word, with convicting and converting power to the glory of Christ.

Believer may suffer *for* Christ.

☐ This form of suffering may include the *involuntary sacrifice* of the *loss of friends, property, reputation, or health.* Voluntary sacrifice or separation **from loved ones, gifts, humiliation, and faithful service, even unto death.**

☐ **Suffering is a gift to the believer.** *For you have been given not only the privilege of trusting in Christ, but also the privilege of suffering for Him.* Philippians 1:29 (NLT).

In suffering with Christ, the Christian may either suffer from man the reproaches of Christ. or he may come to experience with Christ a divinely wrought burden and sorrow for the lost.

☐ Suffering with Christ is a natural phase of a Christian's life and experience (see Romans 9:1-3).

□ It is the love of God shed abroad in our hearts **by the Holy Spirit,** which is given unto us, or in reality, the very love of God reaching out for the lost through the believer (see John 15:12-13; Galatians 5:22).

□ The deepest meaning of suffering with Christ, is to come to experience by the Spirit, an unutterable agony for men out of Christ, and from that vision and love to be willing to offer personal sacrifice or endure physical pain, if need be, that they may be saved.

□ *Taken from: "True Evangelism" by L. S. Chafer*

FACTORS THAT INFLUENCE EVANGELISM
THE HOLY SPIRIT

"He that winneth souls is wise". Proverbs 11:30b (KJV)
"Everyone who has been wise will shine as bright as the sky above, and everyone who has led other to please God will shine like the stars". Daniel 12:3 (CEV

Some facts about the Holy Spirit

Adapted from the *Strong's Concordance and Dake's Annotated Bible*

<u>SUBJECT</u> & <u>SCRIPTURE REFERENCES</u>

Agent in New Birth: (Jn. 3:5-8; Gal. 4:29)

Speaks to men : (Acts 8:29; 10:19)

Directs Gospel work: (Acts 11:12)

Spirit of Holiness: (Rom. 1:14)

Makes free from sin and death: (Rom. 8:1-4)

Imparts love: (Rom. 5:5; 15:30)

Knows the things of God: (I Cor. 2:11)

Makes new creatures in Christ: (I Cor. 6:11; II Cor. 5:17-18)

Baptizes believers into Body of Christ: (I Cor. 12:13)

Gives life: (II Cor. 3:6; Rev. 11:11)

Changes lives to image of Christ: (II Cor. 3:18)

Received by faith, not by works: (Gal. 2:1-5; 14)

Source of hope: (Gal. 5:5)

Imparts character of God: (Gal. 5:22)

Source of true harvest : (Gal. 6:7-10)

Gives access to God: (Eph. 2:18)

Invites men to God: (Rev. 22:17)

Helps men obey truth: (I Peter 1:22)

Helped Christ to make perfect sacrifice for men: (Heb. 9:14)
Renews: (Isa. 32:15)
Convicts men: (Jn 16:8-11)
Guides: (Jn 16:13)
Bears witness: (Rom. 8:16; Heb. 10-15)
Comforts: (Jn 14:16-26)
Gives joy: (Rom. 14:17)
Gives discernment: (I Cor. 2:10-16)
Bears fruit: (Gal. 5:22-23)
Gives gifts: (I Cor. 12:3-11)
Sends out missionaries: (Acts 13:2, 4)
Directs missionaries: (Acts 8:29)

SATAN: THE OBSTACLE WHO HINDERS

1. His work

A. In Relation to Redemptive Work of Christ.

- Tempted Christ (matt. 4:1-11)
- Satan used various people to attempt to thwart work of Christ (Matt. 2:16; 16:23; John 8:44).
- Prediction of conflict (Gen. 3:15)

A. In Relation to Unbelievers

- He blinds their minds (II Cor.4:4).
- Snatches the Word of God from their hearts (Luke 8:12
- Uses men to oppose God's Work (Rev. 2:13)

A. In Relation to the Christian.

- Tempts the Christian to lic (Acts 5:3).
- Accuses and slanders the Christian (Rev. 12:10).
- Hinders the Christian's work (Ithess. 2:18).
- Employs demons in attempts to defeat the Christian (Eph. 6:11-12)
- Incites persecution against the Christian (Rev. 2:10).

1. Original state and fall of Satan.

A. His Privileges and Punishment (See Ezekiel Chapter 28).
B. The Sin (Isaiah 14:13-14).

- I will ascend into heaven.
- I will exalt my throne above the stars of God.
- I will sit on the mount of the assembly in the far north.
- I will ascend above the heights of the clouds (usurp the glory of God)
- I will be like the Most High (possessor of heaven and earth).
- Pride

<u>DIDN'T YOU NOTICE A LOT OF "I WILLS" IN SATAN'S SIN?</u>

ARE YOU SAVED?

<u>DO YOU:</u>

- Recognize that you are a sinner? Romans 3:23

- Understand the penalty of sin? Romans 6:23

- Believe in Jesus? Acts 16:31

- Repent of your sins? Matthew 3:2; Luke 13:3; Acts 2:38

- Confess the Lord Jesus? Romans 10:9-10;
- I John 1:9
- Anchor Yourself in Jesus? Acts 8:36-38;

Romans 4:4;
Romans 3:20-31;
Romans 10:9-13

- Receive God's Grace? Ephesians 2:8-9

ARE YOU SAVED?

ADMIT	YOU NEED TO BE SAVED.
BELIEVE	JESUS DIED ON THE CROSS FOR YOUR SINS.
REPENT	TURN IN THE OPPOSITE DIRECTION FROM SIN.
CONFESS	SAY ALOUD THAT JESUS IS YOUR LORD.
RECEIVE	JESUS BY FAITH AS YOUR PERSONAL LORD AND SAVIOR AND HAVE ETERNAL LIFE.

EXAMPLE

The Result of Salvation

"HE THAT BELIEVETH ON HIM IS NOT CONDEMED: BUT HE THAT BELIEVETH NOT IS CONDEMNED ALREADY, BECAUSE HE HATH NOT BELIEVED IN THE NAME OF THE ONLY BEGOTTEN SON OF GOD. JOHN 3:18

EXAMPLE

WILLIE A. GLASTER, JR.

SESSION ONE
AN INTRODUCTION

WHY EVANGELISM?
CORRECTING THE ASSUMPTION-MAN: A
THREE-PART CREATURE (SPIRITUAL,
NATURAL & CARNAL)

ARE YOU SAVED?

SESSION TWO
THE SOUL WINNER

OBSTACLES THAT HINDER

- Satan: A Defeated Fow
- Methods
- Reasons why people don't receive Jesus Christ
- The Holy Spirit in Evangelism
- Prayer Life
- A brief look at the Spiritual Gift of Evangelism

SESSION THREE:
REASONS WHY PEOPLE DON'T RECEIVE JESUS CHRIST AS LORD AND SAVIOR:

OBJECTIONS & EXCUSES

I'm Too Bad: Hebrews 7:25; Isaiah 1:18

There's Too Much To

Give Up: Mark 8:36; I John 2:15-17

I'm Afraid I Couldn't

Hold Out: I Peter 1:5; Philippians 1:6

I'm Afraid of What Others

Might Think: Matthew 10:32-33

Not Now, But Some

Other Time: Proverbs 27:1; II Cor 6:2

I'm Doing The Best I Can: James 2:10, Isaiah 53:10

God Will Not Condemn Anyone: John 3:18, 36. Hebrews 9:27

How Do I Know That God: John 6:37; II Peter 3:9

Will Accept Me: I Cor. 2:14; II Cor. 5:7

OBJECTIONS AND EXCUSES
PART TWO

JESUS WASN'T REALLY GOD: Hebrews 1:3; John 10:30

IT DOESN'T SOUND

REASONABLE: Isaiah 55:8-9; I Cor. 1:18, 23

I WILL TAKE MY CHANCES: Hebrews 10:31; Luke 12:16-21

I DON'T BELIEVE IN CHRIST: Romans 3:3; Acts 4:12

WILLIE A. GLASTER, JR.

DO ANY OF THESE EXCUSES OR OBJECTIONS
SOUND FAMILIAR TO YOU

64

METHODS THAT CAN HINDER EVANGELISM

1. Substituting the Church's strength in material elements instead of her true character –the strength in her devotion to God.
2. Reducing the Church to a human institution –popular, natural, fleshly and pleasing to man. Man's view eliminates all of the unpopular principles of the Cross—self-denial, life surrender and separation from the world.
3. Social entertainment for the many, not the edification and pleading for the individual, becomes the desired goal.
4. Ignoring the pastoral and teaching aspects of the Word and replacing it with apparent results that are expected. Evangelistic efforts that are confined to stated times and seasons could lead to the impression that God is only occasionally concerned for the soul.
5. A Church's attempt to regain a position once held, but now lost, through "revival". On the other hand, the Scriptures pre-suppose a continual erect, wakeful and aggressive position for service on behalf of every Christian (See Eph. 6:10-17)
6. Public methods which embarrass people may not only be useless, but also intrusive. The Spirit of God is dishonored in the vain attempt to hasten decisions and secure visible results.
7. Ignoring the objective of evangelism—Salvation.

OTHER INFLUENCES THAT HINDER

a. Satan suggest that the Lord is a hard master and that His promises will fail.

b. He perverts the things which are truly work of God and misemploys miracles to obscure God's glory.

c. Often tries to break the soul down and reduce it to despair. He tells us we will never succeed.

d. His most common and successful device—an unforgiving spirit

a. Satan uses every conceivable means to hold men in subjection to himself and keep them from turning to God. If he fails in this, he tries to kill the believer's testimony and ruin his or her influence for God.

b. Satan tries to get others in a lukewarm condition and if he succeeds, urges them to stay in that condition so that God will cut them off in the end.

c. He dares men to do many things which they would do under ordinary circumstances; and men are foolish enough to think they aren't brave if they don't accept his dares.

d. He makes people think they are missing everything in life if they don't go into all kinds of sins, which in the end will damn their souls.

e. He tries to make people think that there is no joy in

serving the Lord. This is one of his greatest errors. Serving Christ and winning souls who will be thankful forever, pay the greatest dividends and afford the greatest pleasures known.

f. He urges churches and church leaders to make religion a paying proposition by appealing to the rich and influential through lowering the standards of hold living, making salvation easy for all, compromising essentials of the faith, feeding the sheep messages on current events and book reviews, instead of the infallible Word of God.

SATAN: A DEFEATED FOE

- The grand adversary of God and man (Job 1:6)

- Hostile to every good

- Ever seeks to defeat the divine plan of grace toward mankind.

(I Peter 5:8)

- Defeated by Christ at Calvary (Gen. 3;15 AND John 3:8)

- Sterilizes the heart (Mark 4:15)

- Causes spiritual blindness (2 Cor. 4:4)

- Judged already (John 16:11)

- To be cast out of this world (John 12:31)

- A conquered enemy of believers (John 12:31)

- His principal method of attack is by temptation.

- Called: Apollyon (destroyer)

- Beelzebub (lawlessness) A vile, worthless person, reckless of God

- The Devil, Lucifer, and Satan

- **The Word of God is the conquering sword in warfare.**

Aptheker, Herbert. <u>A Documentary History of the Negro People in the United States.</u> New York: Citadel Press, 1969.

Brueggemann, Walter. <u>Biblical Perspectives on Evangelism.</u> Nashville: Abingdon Press, 1993.

Cone, James H. **<u>Speaking the Truth: Ecumenism, Liberation, and Black Theology</u>**. Grand Rapids: William B. Weerdmans Publishing, 1986.

Craddock, Fred B. <u>Preaching.</u> Nashville: Abingdon Press, 1985.

DuBois, W.E.B. <u>The Souls of Black Folk.</u> Chicago: AC. McClurg, 1907.

<u>The Negro Church.</u> Atlanta: Atlanta University Press, 1903.

Foner, Philip S. <u>History of Black Americans: From Africa to the Emergence of the Cotton Kingdom.</u> Westport: Greenwood Press, 1974.

Harkness, Georgia. <u>"Understanding the Christian Faith."</u> <u>Readings In Christian Thought.</u> 2nd ed. Ed. Hugh T. Kerr. Nashville: Abingdon Press, 1990.

Hilkert, Mary C. <u>Naming Grace.</u> Nashville: The Continuum, 1997.

Johnson, James W. <u>The Book of American Negro Poetry.</u> New York: Harcourt Brace Jovanvich, 1969.

King, Jr., Martin L. <u>Why We Can't Wait.</u> New York: Harper & Row, 1964.

Kunjufu, Jawnza. <u>Adam! Where Are You?</u> Chicago: African American Images, 1994.

Long, Thomas G. <u>The Witness of Preaching.</u> Louisville:

Westminster John Knox, 1989.

Meeks, Wayne A. <u>The Harper Collins Study Bible: New Revised Standard Version.</u> New York: Harper Collins Publishers, 1993.

Montgomery, William E. <u>"Under Their Own Vine and Fig Tree: The African American Church In the South</u>, 1865-1970." 19 Feb. 2006. <http://www.tsha.utexas.edu/handbook/online/articles/[1] AA/ pkatz print.html>

Paris, Peter J. "Black Theology and Pastoral Care." <u>Dictionary of Pastoral Care and Counseling.</u> Ed. Rodney J. Hunter. Nashville: Abingdon Press, 1990.

Riggs, Charles and Tom Phillips. <u>The Billy Graham Christian Life & Witness Course</u>. Minneapolis: Billy Graham Evangelistic Association, 1990.

Robertson, Edwin H. <u>"No Rusty Swords"</u> Collected Works of Dietrich Bonhoeffer. New York: Harper & Row, 1947.

Southard, Samuel S. and Anita Ostrom. <u>"Evangelizing".</u> <u>Dictionary of Pastoral Care and Counseling</u>. Ed. Rodney J. Hunter. Nashville: Abingdon Press, 1990.

Stagg, Frank. <u>New Testament Theology.</u> Nashville: Broadman Press, 1962.

Stock, Augustine. <u>"Witness." The Collegeville Pastoral Dictionary of Biblical Theology</u>. Ed. Carroll Stuhlmueller. Collegeville: The Liturgical Press, 1996.

Thompson, William G. <u>"Good News/Gospel".The Collegeville Pastoral Dictionary of Biblical Theology.</u> Ed. Carroll Stuhlrnueller.

---

1. http://www.tsha.utexas.edu/handbook/online/articles/

Collegeville: Liturgical Press, 1996.

Throckmorton, Burton H. Gospel Parallels: A Comparison of the Synoptic Gospels. 5th ed.

Nashville: Thomas Nelson, Inc., 1992.

Vine, W. E. Vine's Expository Dictionary of New Testament Words. Westwood: Barbour and Company, 1952.

Walker, T. Vaughn and Robert Smith, Jr. "Christian Ministry in the African American Church".

Preparing for Christian Ministry. Ed. David P. Gushee and Walter C. Jackson. Wheaton: Victor Books, 1996.

Wilmore, Garraud S. and James H. Cone. Black Theology: A Documentary, 1966-1979.

Maryknoll: Orbis Books, 1979

Spurgeon, Charles, H., Satan: A Defeated Foe

Whitaker House, 1993

Spurgeon, C., H., The Soul Winner: "he that winneth souls is wise".

Whitaker House, 1995

McClellan, Albert, The Missions Tasks of a Church

Convention Press, Nashville, Tennessee, 1969

Bethel A.M.E Church, Evangelism Workshop, 2001, San Antonio, TX

Works adapted from various sources in this bibliography.

Coleman, Robert, E. with Study Guide by Fish, Roy, J.,

Foreword by Billy Graham, The Master Plan of Evangelism

Fleming H. Revell Company, 1972

Epp, Theodore, The Other Comforter: Practical on the Holy Spirit

The Good News Broadcasting Association, Inc., 1966, 1983

Chafer, Lewis, Sperry, True Evangelism: Winning Souls
Through Prayer
Kregel Publications, Grand Rapids, MI, 1993
The Spirit-filled Christian: Design for Discipleship
by The Navigators, 1973
Blackaby, Henry and Richard, King, Claude, Experiencing God:
Knowing and Doing The Will of God
Lifeway Press, Nashville, TN, 2007
Weston, Owen, C., Spiritual Gifts: You Job Description from
God.
LifeSprings Resources, 1996

Friendship Baptist Church, Vacation Bible School, 1996,
San Antonio, TX, 1996l. Works adapted from sources:
In this bibliography.

Don't miss out!

Visit the website below and you can sign up to receive emails whenever Willie A. Glaster, Jr. publishes a new book. There's no charge and no obligation.

https://books2read.com/r/B-A-VGLDB-MTBXC

BOOKS2READ

Connecting independent readers to independent writers.

www.ingramcontent.com/pod-product-compliance
Lightning Source LLC
Chambersburg PA
CBHW031447130726

47989CB00003B/1306